THE VOICE IN YOUR HEAD—
The LoopBreaker Journal

A Journal for Breaking Loops and Becoming

by *Noah Wraith*

Healing isn't easy but this journal can be.

First Edition · OneVoiceOS LLC·
Dothan, Alabama · 2025

THE VOICE IN YOUR HEAD —
THE LOOPBREAKER JOURNAL

The Voice in Your Head — The LoopBreaker Journal
First Edition · 2025
Dothan, Alabama

Copyright © 2025 by Noah Wraith
All rights assigned to OneVoiceOS LLC
Published by OneVoiceOS LLC
Printed in the United States

All rights reserved. No part of this book may be reproduced, stored in a retrieval system, or transmitted in any form or by any means—electronic, mechanical, photocopying, recording, or otherwise—without prior written permission of the publisher, except in the case of brief quotations used in critical articles or reviews.

ISBN: 979-8-9993026-2-5

This journal is not intended to replace professional therapy, counseling, or medical treatment. If you are struggling with mental health issues, please seek support from a qualified professional.

Table of Contents

The Quiet Before the Becoming……………………………1

How to Use This Journal…………………………………3

Why Your Brain Feels Like a Dark Carnival……………5

Section 1 – The Unraveling (Days 1-30)………………..7

Section 2 – The Reckoning (Days 31-60)……………...69

Section 3 – The Becoming(Days 61-90)……………....131

Final Reflection Ritual……………………………….193

This is Not the End…………………………………….195

LoopBreaker Next Steps………………………..197

THE QUIET BEFORE THE BECOMING

This isn't healing.
This isn't a process.
It's a reckoning.

Before you start writing, before you try to fix anything, I want you to understand this: You're not broken. You're buried.

Beneath the loops.
Beneath the masks.
Beneath the noise.

This journal isn't here to solve you.
It's here to show you.
To mirror you.

To let you see the version of you that's been waiting.
Take a breath.
This is the quiet before the becoming.

Let's begin.

HOW TO USE THIS JOURNAL

This isn't a workbook.

It's not a checklist. Or a challenge.

It's a ritual.

A mirror.

A reckoning.

Each day, you'll find a few short reflections. Sometimes it's a question. Sometimes it's a challenge. Sometimes it's a reminder.

After that, there's space.

Use it.

You're not here to answer me.

You're here to answer yourself.

Here's how this works:

Show up.

Read the reflection.

Write what's true.

Some days that's a sentence. Some days it's a scream. Both count.

Keep going.

There's no prize for finishing every page.

But every page you meet yourself on is a loop you can break.

This is your ritual.

This is your mirror.

Let's begin.

WHY YOUR BRAIN FEELS LIKE A DARK CARNIVAL

Your nervous system isn't working against you. It's working too hard to protect you.

When your brain thinks you're in danger—emotional, physical, or otherwise—it stops asking what's real. It starts repeating what's familiar.

Imagine your mind as a carnival.

But not the bright, happy kind.

This one's dim.
The lights flicker.
The music sounds warped, but familiar.

Everything feels off.

The Ringmaster? That's your survival self. Running the show. Keeping you moving, no matter how tired you are.

The Masks? They're everywhere. Performers you don't recognize. Identities you've worn so long you've forgotten your real face.

The Haunted House? That's your loops. Same hallways. Same fears. Same exit you never find.

That's your nervous system running the show.

It's not broken.

It's just stuck.

This journal helps you step out of the carnival.

Each time you write, each time you name a mask or a loop, your brain does something incredible:

It rewires.

That's neuroplasticity.

That's healing.

That's how you reclaim your voice—not overnight, but one reflection at a time.

Ready?

Let's start turning the lights back on.

Part 1
THE UNRAVELING

This is where the masks crack.
Where the loops become visible.
Where the pretending starts to fall apart.
You're not here to fix yourself.
You're here to see yourself.
This is the beginning.
Not of healing.
But of honesty.
Let's start.

DAY 1

Where Are You Now?

Before you write, pause.
Where are you? Not physically. Inside.
Don't give me the easy answer—not "sad," not "tired," not "fine." Those are surface words. Look underneath.
Are you hollow? Anxious? Detached? Are you waiting for someone to notice you've disappeared?
Don't overthink it. Just notice.

Reflective Prompts:

Prompt 1:
Where are you right now—not physically, but inside? What does it feel like to be here?
(Describe the feeling, not just the label.)

Prompt 2:
What's underneath that feeling? Where do you think it came from?

Prompt 3:
What's something you wish you'd said today, but you held it in—for the sake of being okay?

Breathe. You're here. That's the start.

**Whatever needs to come out—let it.
There's no wrong answer.**

DAY 2

What Story Are You Repeating?

Every loop has a story.
Sometimes it sounds like:
"I'll never get this right."
"I'm too much."
"I don't need anyone."
Your brain doesn't repeat those stories to hurt you. It repeats them to protect you.
But protection isn't peace. Today, you're going to name the story—not to fix it, just to see it.
Because what you can see, you can eventually choose to leave.

Reflective Prompts:

Prompt 1:
What's the story you keep telling yourself when things get hard?

Prompt 2:
Where do you think that story came from? (Whose voice taught you to believe it?)

Prompt 3:
What would change if you stopped believing that story?

Breathe. You're not wrong for surviving. But survival isn't the goal anymore.

**Whatever needs to come out—let it.
There's no wrong answer.**

DAY 3

What Role Are You Playing?

Every story has a role. When life gets heavy, you step into yours. Maybe you become the Fixer. Maybe the Silent One. Maybe the Person Who's Fine.
You don't choose that role on purpose.
It's what your nervous system thinks keeps you safe.
Today isn't about blaming that. It's about noticing it.

Reflective Prompts:

Prompt 1:
When life feels heavy, who do you become?

Prompt 2:
What do you think that role protects you from?

Prompt 3:
What would it feel like to stop performing that role—even for a moment?

Breathe.
You're not wrong for surviving.
But you're allowed to choose something else.

**Whatever needs to come out—let it.
There's no wrong answer.**

DAY 4

What Does "Safe" Feel Like?

We talk about safety like it's simple. But for some of us, "safe" means being invisible. Or quiet. Or never needing anything at all. Sometimes we mistake comfort for safety. Sometimes we think control is the only version of safety we're allowed to have.

But safety isn't the absence of chaos. It's the presence of honesty.

Today isn't about having the right answer.

It's about seeing what safety actually feels like in your body—not what you *wish* it felt like, but what it really means for you right now.

Reflective Prompts:

Prompt 1:
What do you usually call "safe"? (Comfort? Numbness? Silence? Control? Be honest.)

Prompt 2:
When was the last time you truly felt safe—if ever?

Prompt 3:
What would safety feel like if it wasn't tied to performance or control?

Breathe. You deserve real safety. Not the kind you have to earn.

**Whatever needs to come out—let it.
There's no wrong answer.**

DAY 5

When Did You Start Pretending?

Everyone wears a mask. But no one's born with one.
We pick it up when being real stops feeling safe.
Sometimes it happens slowly.
Other times it's sharp—one moment, one wound, one betrayal that tells you:
"Don't show them who you really are. It's not safe."
This isn't about blame. It's about memory.
Today is about finding the moment the mask began to matter.

Reflective Prompts:

Prompt 1:
When did you first learn it wasn't safe to be fully seen?

Prompt 2:
What part of yourself did you start hiding first?

Prompt 3:
What did pretending protect you from?

Breathe. You don't have to keep performing

**Whatever needs to come out—let it.
There's no wrong answer.**

DAY 6

What Happens When You're Seen?

Some of us want to be seen—desperately.
Others have learned that being seen means being judged, abandoned, or misunderstood.
Sometimes we think we want connection, but deep down, we fear it.
Because being seen means being vulnerable. And vulnerable hasn't always been safe.
Today is about noticing what rises in you when you're visible.
Not what you think should happen—
but what your body does when someone actually looks at you and really sees you.

Reflective Prompts:

Prompt 1:
What feelings come up when you think about being fully seen—emotionally, not just physically?

Prompt 2:
What memories taught you that visibility was unsafe?

Prompt 3:
If someone truly saw the real you, what do you fear they would see?

Breathe. You're not too much. You're just not used to being fully witnessed

**Whatever needs to come out—let it.
There's no wrong answer.**

DAY 7

Loop Pause: What Are You Starting to See?

One week in.
Not everything has landed yet—and that's okay.
You don't have to understand every loop to start noticing the pull.
Today is not about "fixing." It's about witnessing.
Step back.
Look gently at what's been rising. Don't judge. Don't rush.
Just notice the patterns.

Reflective Prompts:

Prompt 1:
What themes or phrases have repeated in your writing this week?

Prompt 2:
Have any roles, masks, or feelings shown up more than once?

Prompt 3:
What's the loop you're beginning to notice—but still avoiding?

Breathe. You're not behind. You're exactly where you're meant to pause.

**Whatever needs to come out—let it.
There's no wrong answer.**

DAY 8

Who Did You Have to Become?

Sometimes, the person we are today isn't the person we chose to be.
It's the person we *had* to become to survive where we came from.
Maybe you learned to be strong, quiet, funny, perfect, invisible.
Not because it was you— But because it kept you safe.
Kept you loved. Kept you from falling apart.
This isn't about judgment. It's about recognition.
Before you can become something new, you need to see what you've been rehearsing all this time.

Reflective Prompts:

Prompt 1:
What traits or roles did you adopt to survive the environment you grew up in?

Prompt 2:
Do those traits still serve you—or are they starting to feel heavy?

Prompt 3:
If you didn't have to protect yourself anymore, who might you become?

Breathe. You're allowed to change—even if it kept you safe.

**Whatever needs to come out—let it.
There's no wrong answer.**

DAY 9

Who Do They Think You Are?

Every room you've ever walked into, someone formed a story about you.
Sometimes you played into it. Sometimes you fought it.
Sometimes you let them believe it because it felt easier than correcting them.
But there's a cost to being misunderstood. To being edited.
To watching people respond to a version of you that isn't real.
Today isn't about fixing perception.
It's about naming the gap between how they see you—and how you see yourself.

Reflective Prompts:

Prompt 1:
When people describe you, what traits or labels do they use?

Prompt 2:
Which parts of that feel real—and which parts feel like performance?

Prompt 3:
What's something true about you that people often miss or never see?

Breathe. You're not invisible. You've just been filtered.

**Whatever needs to come out—let it.
There's no wrong answer.**

DAY 10

What Did It Cost?

Every time you silenced your truth— To keep the peace.
To protect someone else. To avoid the fallout.
You paid something.
Sometimes it was your voice. Sometimes your boundaries.
Sometimes your sense of self.
Not all survival strategies feel like choices. But every loop comes with a cost.
Today, you name it—not to punish yourself, but to honor what it took to make it here.

Reflective Prompts:

Prompt 1:
What have you lost—or put aside—to stay safe in your relationships?

Prompt 2:
What's something you haven't allowed yourself to say out loud, even to yourself?

Prompt 3:
What would it mean to reclaim the part of you that you left behind?

Breathe. The cost wasn't your fault. But reclaiming is your right.

**Whatever needs to come out—let it.
There's no wrong answer.**

DAY 11

What Have You Been Swallowing?

There are things you've wanted to say.
Moments you felt the truth rise to your lips—and you buried it.
Not because you were weak.
Because you were wired to keep the peace.
To stay small. To avoid what comes next.
Sometimes the silence hurts more than the thing you didn't say.
This isn't about guilt. It's about gravity. Every swallowed truth becomes weight.
Today, you name what's been heavy.

Reflective Prompts:

Prompt 1:
What's something you've been holding back—out of fear, habit, or loyalty?

Prompt 2:
What did it cost you to stay silent?

Prompt 3:
If you were to say the truth—even just here—what would come out?

Breathe. The weight was never meant to stay inside you.

**Whatever needs to come out—let it.
There's no wrong answer.**

DAY 12

What's Your Role in the Loop?

Every loop has a cast.
Sometimes you're the rescuer. Sometimes the peacekeeper.
Sometimes the one who disappears.
It's not always your fault. But it is your pattern.
And it is your job to recognize it.
Naming your role doesn't mean blaming yourself.
It means reclaiming your place in the story.
It means taking responsibility of it.

Reflective Prompts:

Prompt 1:
When conflict happens, who do you become?

Prompt 2:
What do you tend to take responsibility for—even when it isn't yours?

Prompt 3:
What would it mean to step out of that role?

Breathe. Patterns can be rewritten. But only if you name the part you've been playing.

**Whatever needs to come out—let it.
There's no wrong answer.**

DAY 13

What Part of You Feels Untouchable?

Everyone has a place inside they protect.
Sometimes it's shame. Sometimes grief.
Sometimes a truth that never had room to exist.
You may not talk about it. You may not even look at it often.
But you feel it.
This isn't about dragging it into the light.
Just acknowledging that it's there.
And that it matters.

Reflective Prompts:

Prompt 1:
What's the part of you that feels off-limits—even to yourself?

Prompt 2:
What made you hide it?

Prompt 3:
What would it take to let it breathe?

Breathe. Even the quietest parts of you deserve a voice.

**Whatever needs to come out—let it.
There's no wrong answer.**

DAY 14
Ritual Letter: To the One Who Disappeared

This isn't a prompt.
It's a reckoning.

You're going to write a letter to the version of you who vanished.
The one who swallowed their truth.
Who gave up their voice.
Who tried to earn love by becoming smaller.

Not to blame them.
But to witness them.
You can thank them.
You can scream at them.
You can hold them.
Just don't ignore them.

Write to the version of you who first put on the mask.

What were they afraid of?
What did they want?
What did they never get to say?
You don't have to send it.
You just have to write it.
Be honest.
Honesty with yourself is the most powerful tool you have.

Use the next page to write the letter.

This isn't for anyone else.
This is for the part of you that never got to speak.

Breathe.
This is grief.
This is healing.
This is how you come back.

This page is for the part of you that disappeared.

DAY 15

Who Taught You Love Meant Earning It?

You weren't born thinking you had to earn love.
That came later. Maybe from silence.
Maybe from approval that only showed up when you did something "right."
For some of us, love became a transaction. Affection for performance. Connection for self-erasure.
But love isn't supposed to cost you yourself.

Reflective Prompts:

Prompt 1:
What moments taught you that love had to be earned?

Prompt 2:
What did you do—or stop doing—to stay loved?

Prompt 3:
If love didn't require performance, what would it look like?

Breathe. You don't have to keep trading yourself away.

**Whatever needs to come out—let it.
There's no wrong answer.**

DAY 16

When Did You Stop Asking for What You Needed?

Somewhere along the way, you stopped reaching out.
Stopped saying, "That hurt." Stopped asking, "Can you see me?"
Stopped being real about your needs.
Maybe no one listened. Maybe it just felt safer not to need.
But you still have needs. And silence doesn't make them go away.
It just buries them deeper.

Reflective Prompts:

Prompt 1:
When did you first learn that asking for your needs was risky or pointless?

Prompt 2:
What's a need you still haven't let yourself name?

Prompt 3:
What would it feel like to say it now—even just here?

Breathe. You don't have to apologize for needing.

**Whatever needs to come out—let it.
There's no wrong answer.**

DAY 17

What Are You Still Apologizing For?

Not always with words.
Sometimes with over-explaining. Sometimes with shrinking.
Sometimes by trying to make everything easier for everyone but you.
When you're used to blame, you start carrying guilt that doesn't belong to you.
But not everything that went wrong was your fault.

Reflective Prompts:

Prompt 1:
What parts of yourself are you still apologizing for—directly or indirectly?

Prompt 2:
Whose reactions taught you to feel guilty for being you?

Prompt 3:
What would change if you stopped apologizing for existing?

Breathe. You're allowed to take up space.

**Whatever needs to come out—let it.
There's no wrong answer.**

DAY 18

What Parts of You Still Feel Unwanted?

There are parts of you you've tried to cut off.
Parts that felt "too much," or "not enough," or "the reason they left."
You didn't get rid of them.
You just hid them.
You made them quiet.
But they're still in there—waiting to be reclaimed.
You don't need to amputate parts of yourself to be worthy of love.

Reflective Prompts:

Prompt 1:
What traits or emotions have you learned to hide to be accepted?

Prompt 2:
When did you first start feeling like those parts made you "unlovable"?

Prompt 3:
What would it feel like to stop hiding them?

Breathe. Nothing about you is too much for the right place.

**Whatever needs to come out—let it.
There's no wrong answer.**

DAY 19

What's the Script You Keep Falling Back Into?

Even after awareness, even after insight, the old script tries to take over.
It says:
"Don't rock the boat."
"Don't get attached."
"Don't ask for more."
"Just survive."
That voice isn't you.
It's your history trying to stay in control.
Today, you're going to name the script.
So it stops running the show.

Reflective Prompts:

Prompt 1:
What are the familiar thoughts or phrases that repeat when you're triggered or afraid?

Prompt 2:
Whose voice do they sound like?

Prompt 3:
What's a new line you could write—one that belongs to you?

Breathe. You're not doomed to keep rehearsing the same role.

**Whatever needs to come out—let it.
There's no wrong answer.**

DAY 20

What Are You Tired of Pretending?

Pretending keeps things in place.
It keeps relationships calm. It keeps expectations met.
But it also keeps *you* on hold.
You've been pretending longer than you realize.
To be fine.
To be functional.
To be someone they can count on—at the cost of counting on yourself.
Pretending isn't peace.
It's a slow erosion.

Reflective Prompts:

Prompt 1:
What have you been pretending not to feel?

Prompt 2:
What role or identity do you perform even when it hurts?

Prompt 3:
What truth would disrupt the system around you if you said it out loud?

Breathe. The truth won't ruin everything. But pretending might.

**Whatever needs to come out—let it.
There's no wrong answer.**

DAY 21

Loop Pause: What's Starting to Feel Familiar?

You're three weeks in.
And by now, certain patterns are showing up again—thoughts, emotions, reactions.
That's not failure.
That's visibility.
Loops don't disappear overnight.
They reveal themselves when you're finally still enough to see them.
This is your moment to track them.
Not to fix them. Just to name them.

Reflective Prompts:

Prompt 1:
What patterns or thoughts have started repeating during this process?

Prompt 2:
Where do you feel them show up in your body?

Prompt 3:
What part of you is trying to stay in control—and why?

Breathe. Loops are louder right before they break.

**Whatever needs to come out—let it.
There's no wrong answer.**

DAY 22

What Part of You Is Still Performing?

You've done the work.
You've taken the mask off—at least a little.
But performance has layers.
Sometimes it sounds like a fake laugh.
Sometimes it looks like saying "I'm good" when you're not.
Sometimes it's agreeing just to keep the peace.
It's okay. The performance served a purpose.
But now you get to ask:
Do I still need it?

Reflective Prompts:

Prompt 1:
Where in your life are you still performing—masking how you actually feel?

Prompt 2:
What fear is keeping the performance alive?

Prompt 3:
What would it look like to let the real version of you speak instead?

Breathe. You're not here to be palatable. You're here to be real.

**Whatever needs to come out—let it.
There's no wrong answer.**

DAY 23

Who Did You Learn to Protect?

Sometimes the mask wasn't for you.
It was for them.
Maybe you stayed silent to protect a parent.
Maybe you became "easy" so your partner didn't have to face themselves.
Maybe you hid your pain because someone else needed you strong.
But protection isn't connection.
And self-erasure doesn't save anyone.
It just hurts you.

Reflective Prompts:

Prompt 1:
Who in your life have you tried to protect by hiding your own truth?

Prompt 2:
What did it cost you to carry what wasn't yours?

Prompt 3:
What would happen if you let yourself be seen—even if it disrupted their comfort?

Breathe. You don't have to carry what was never yours to hold.

**Whatever needs to come out—let it.
There's no wrong answer.**

DAY 24

What Have You Been Waiting For?

You've held back.
Maybe for the right time.
Maybe for someone to choose you.
Maybe because it never felt safe to move forward alone.
But here you are—still waiting.
And underneath that waiting is a question:
What are you afraid might happen if you finally moved?
This isn't about blame.
It's about reclaiming the time you've been stuck at the edge.

Reflective Prompts:

Prompt 1:
What part of your life feels like it's been "on pause"?

Prompt 2:
What have you been waiting for—permission, safety, certainty?

Prompt 3:
What would it feel like to take one step without waiting anymore?

Breathe. You don't need to earn forward motion. You're allowed to begin.

**Whatever needs to come out—let it.
There's no wrong answer.**

DAY 25

What Do You Keep Going Back to?

It might not make sense.
It might not be good for you.
But you keep circling back.
To a person. To a habit.
To a story about yourself.
You don't return because you're weak.
You return because it's *familiar*.
Even when it hurts.
Today, we name what you keep orbiting—so you can decide if you're ready to land somewhere new.

Reflective Prompts:

Prompt 1:
What's something or someone you keep returning to, even when it doesn't serve you?

Prompt 2:
What feeling are you chasing when you go back?

Prompt 3:
What are you afraid would happen if you let it go?

Breathe. You don't have to stay loyal to your suffering.

**Whatever needs to come out—let it.
There's no wrong answer.**

DAY 26

What Keeps You From Saying the Truth Out Loud?
You've written a lot.
Maybe you've uncovered things you didn't know were in there.
But speaking truth isn't the same as writing it.
Writing is a whisper. Speaking is a rupture.
And somewhere in you, there's a truth that *wants* to be said.
But also a fear that keeps it locked away.

Reflective Prompts:
Prompt 1:
What's a truth you've uncovered during this process that you still haven't said out loud?

Prompt 2:
What's the fear that rises when you imagine saying it?

Prompt 3:
Who would be most affected if you told the truth—and why does that matter?

Breathe. You don't have to shout it. But it deserves to exist outside of you.

**Whatever needs to come out—let it.
There's no wrong answer.**

DAY 27

What Almost Breaks the Loop?

Not everything that hurts is a trap.
Some of it's *almost* a breakthrough.
A moment of courage that you walk away from.
A question you ask yourself, then bury again.
A boundary you almost speak—but don't.
Those moments matter.
They're the edges of change.
Today, you name the moment you keep *almost* crossing—so next time, you can step through.

Reflective Prompts:

Prompt 1:
What's a moment or decision that you keep circling but never quite commit to?

Prompt 2:
What part of you pulls back at the last second—and what is it trying to protect?

Prompt 3:
What might change if you stepped through the next time?

Breathe. Almost breaking the loop means you're close. Very close.

**Whatever needs to come out—let it.
There's no wrong answer.**

DAY 28

Ritual Letter: To the One Who Performed

You've worn the mask so well, you forgot where your real face was.
You smiled when you wanted to scream.
You made yourself likable, needed, impressive, easy.
You called it strength.
But it was survival.
The Performer kept you safe.
They kept you loved—maybe even alive.
But now you're here.
And maybe you don't need them anymore.
Today, you write to the one who kept showing up so you wouldn't fall apart.
This letter isn't a goodbye.
It's a thank you.
And maybe, a release.

Use the next page to write a letter to the version of you who performed to survive.

What were they afraid would happen if they stopped?
What did they sacrifice to keep you protected?
What do you want to say to them now?

You don't have to perform here.
Just be honest.

Breathe.

This is the shift.
This is the permission.
This is where you choose to be seen.

This page is for the part of you that's been performing.

DAY 29

What Are You Ready to Leave Behind?

You've been unraveling for four weeks.
You've named the loops. You've seen the masks.
You've spoken to the parts of you that stayed hidden for years.
Now the question becomes:
What are you done carrying?
This isn't about fixing it all.
It's about letting something go—maybe for the first time.

Reflective Prompts:

Prompt 1:
What belief, pattern, or mask are you ready to stop holding onto?

Prompt 2:
What part of you is still afraid to let it go?

Prompt 3:
If you walked forward without it, what would you make room for?

Breathe. Every ending is a space waiting to be filled.

**Whatever needs to come out—let it.
There's no wrong answer.**

DAY 30

Mirror Page: Who Are You Becoming?

Look back.
Really look.
The version of you who started this journal didn't know how much they were holding.
Now you do.
You've survived.
You've softened.
You've stared straight into the patterns that have shaped your life.
But you're not just unraveling anymore.
You're becoming.
Today, this page is for the one you're stepping into.
Not the perfect version.
Not the healed one.
The one who's honest.
Present.
Willing to move forward without pretending.

Mirror Letter

Write a letter or a vow to the version of you who you want to become.
You don't need to be them yet.
But you're already on the way.

Breathe.
You made it through the unraveling.
Now you know what was never really yours to carry.

This page is for the version of you that's waiting to arrive.

PART 2
THE RECKONING

This is where things get loud.

The Unraveling let's you name what was broken.
The Reckoning asks what you're still holding on to—and why.
This is the part most people avoid.

The grief.
The shame.
The resistance.

You might want to skip days.
You might get angry at the page.

That's okay.
Anger is part of it.
So is fear.

You're not here to perform.
You're here to face the patterns that never served you—but became your story anyway.

This part doesn't fix you.
It frees you.
One truth at a time.

DAY 31

What Have You Been Avoiding?

You've named the loops. You've seen the masks.
You've told the truth on paper more than some people do in a lifetime.
But this part—the reckoning—isn't about seeing. It's about *staying*.
Staying with the discomfort. Staying with the silence.
Staying with the part of you that already knows what needs to change…
but keeps putting it off.
So today, we begin here: Not with what hurts— but with what you've been *avoiding*.
Because what we avoid *owns* us. And what we face, even briefly, begins to lose its grip.

Reflective Prompts:
Prompt 1:
What part of your life have you been most avoiding looking at?

Prompt 2:
What does your avoidance protect you from—and what does it *cost* you?

Prompt 3:
If you weren't afraid to face it… what would your first step be?

Breathe. Avoidance is not failure. It's just a signal that something matters.
And you're finally strong enough to face it.

**Whatever needs to come out—let it.
There's no wrong answer.**

DAY 32

Who Did You Inherit This From?

Most of what we call ourselves was handed to us before we could speak.
Beliefs. Fears. Patterns. Roles.
We didn't choose them—
we absorbed them.
And then we survived with them.
But just because you inherited something doesn't mean you have to keep carrying it.
Today is about identifying the hand-me-downs.
The patterns that never really belonged to you—
but shaped you anyway.

Reflective Prompts:

Prompt 1:
What belief or behavior feels like it didn't start with you?

Prompt 2:
Who might you have inherited that from? (A parent, a caregiver, a culture, a relationship?)

Prompt 3:
Do you want to keep carrying it? Why or why not?

Breathe. You are allowed to question what you were taught. That's how you start becoming who you are.

**Whatever needs to come out—let it.
There's no wrong answer.**

DAY 33

What Part of You Still Wants to Be Chosen?

Even the strongest people ache to be seen.
Not just for what they do. But for who they are.
Sometimes we say we don't care. Sometimes we pretend we don't need anyone.
But deep underneath, there's still a part of us— a younger part—
waiting for someone to choose us.
To say:
"I see you. I pick you. You're not too much."
Today is about finding that part.
Not to shame it. But to sit beside it. And maybe, for the first time, choose yourself.

Reflective Prompts:

Prompt 1:
What's one memory where you felt like you weren't chosen?

Prompt 2:
What part of you still wants to be picked, seen, or prioritized?

Prompt 3:
What would it look like to give that to yourself today?

Breathe. You're not needy. You're human. And you are worth choosing.

**Whatever needs to come out—let it.
There's no wrong answer.**

DAY 34

What Did You Learn to Perform?

Not all masks are lies. Some are survival.
You learned to be *pleasing* so you wouldn't be abandoned.
You learned to be *strong* so no one would see you fall apart.
You learned to be *funny* so no one would ask if you were okay.
Performance isn't fake—it's adaptive.
But it comes at a cost.
Today, we look at what you perform…
and ask what's underneath it.

Reflective Prompts:

Prompt 1:
What parts of your personality feel like performance rather than presence?

Prompt 2:
What did you get in return for performing that role?

Prompt 3:
What would happen if you stopped?

Breathe. This isn't about dropping everything all at once.
It's about noticing what's real—and what you're ready to release.

**Whatever needs to come out—let it.
There's no wrong answer.**

DAY 35

When Did You Stop Trusting Yourself?

You weren't always this doubtful.
This second-guessing.
This unsure.
There was a time—maybe long ago—when your instincts were intact.
When your "yes" was yours.
When your "no" was clear.
When your voice didn't shake from trying to say the *right* thing instead of the *real* thing.
Today is about tracing the fracture.
The moment (or moments) where your trust in yourself cracked.
And beginning to gather the pieces.

Reflective Prompts:

Prompt 1:
Can you remember a time when you trusted yourself—fully? What changed?

Prompt 2:
Was there a person, event, or pattern that made you question your voice?

Prompt 3:
What would trusting yourself again look like today, in one small way?

Breathe. Trust doesn't come back all at once. But today… you can start listening.

**Whatever needs to come out—let it.
There's no wrong answer.**

DAY 36

Loop Pause: The Pattern That Still Pulls You

Take a breath. Step back.
This isn't a day to fix anything. It's a day to see. You've been doing the work.
Writing the words. Tracing the threads. Now ask yourself: What pattern keeps pulling you back?
Maybe it's silence. Or over-explaining.
Or choosing people who make you feel small.
Whatever it is—it's not random. It's a loop.
And today, we pause to name it.

Reflective Prompts:

Prompt 1:
What's one emotional loop you've noticed repeating since this journal began?

Prompt 2:
Where does it usually start? What triggers it?

Prompt 3:
What do you think this loop is trying to protect you from?

Breathe. You're not here to break the loop in one day.
You're here to see it clearly—so it doesn't run you silently.

**Whatever needs to come out—let it.
There's no wrong answer.**

DAY 37

When Did You First Feel Responsible for Someone Else's Emotions?

This one might hit hard.
Somewhere along the line,
you learned to track other people's moods like a survival skill.
You adjusted.
Softened. Performed. Disappeared.
Not because you wanted to—but because it felt safer to manage them than to express you.
Today's about tracing that moment.
The origin of emotional responsibility that was never yours to carry.

Reflective Prompts:

Prompt 1:
What's your first memory of feeling responsible for someone else's feelings?

Prompt 2:
How did that moment change how you expressed your own emotions?

Prompt 3:
What would it feel like to let that responsibility go—even just a little?

Breathe. You don't have to keep holding what was never yours.

**Whatever needs to come out—let it.
There's no wrong answer.**

DAY 38

What Part of You Still Believes You Deserve the Pain?

Be honest with yourself.
There's a part of you—buried deep—that still thinks the pain was earned.
That maybe you were too much.
Too loud.
Too sensitive.
Too broken.
It's not true.
But until you name it, it runs you.
So today, we ask:
What part of you still holds the shame?

Reflective Prompts:

Prompt 1:
When pain shows up, do you ever feel like you deserved it? Where do you think that belief comes from?

Prompt 2:
What message did you internalize about your worth?

Prompt 3:
If you could speak to that part of you—the one still carrying the shame—what would you say?

Breathe. You're not your pain. You're what survived it.

**Whatever needs to come out—let it.
There's no wrong answer.**

DAY 39

What Did You Learn You Had to Be?

Before you had a voice, you had a role.
Maybe you became the quiet one.
The helper.
The achiever.
Maybe you smiled when it hurt. Stayed calm when you were crumbling.
You learned how to earn love by being less of a burden.
But roles are not identities.
They're costumes we wear to survive.
So today we ask:
What did you learn you had to be—and what did it cost you?

Reflective Prompts:

Prompt 1:
What role did you play in your early relationships—family, school, or friends?

Prompt 2:
How did that role protect you? What did it prevent you from expressing?

Prompt 3:
What part of yourself had to disappear so you could keep playing that role?

Breathe. You don't have to perform to be worthy. You're allowed to be seen as you are.

**Whatever needs to come out—let it.
There's no wrong answer.**

DAY 40

Who Taught You That Silence Was Safer?

There's a moment you stopped speaking.
Not out loud—but from the inside.
A moment you swallowed what you needed to scream.
To keep the peace. To stay loved. To stay safe.
Maybe it wasn't one moment. Maybe it was many.
But silence leaves a scar.
And healing starts when you name where it came from.
So today we ask:
Who taught you that silence was the only way to survive?

Reflective Prompts:

Prompt 1:
What's the earliest memory you have of holding something in?

Prompt 2:
Who made you feel like your truth was "too much"? What did you stop saying?

Prompt 3:
If you could go back and speak the truth in that moment—what would you say now?

Breathe. Your voice is still in there. This time, let it come out.

**Whatever needs to come out—let it.
There's no wrong answer.**

DAY 41

What Did You Do to Survive That You No Longer Need?

We adapt to pain in brilliant ways.
We shrink. We perform.
We disappear.
We become what the world will allow.
But survival isn't the same as living.
And not everything that once kept you safe still belongs in the life you're building.
So today, ask yourself:
What survival pattern are you still carrying—long after it served its purpose?

Reflective Prompts:

Prompt 1:
What did you have to do to stay emotionally safe when you were younger?

Prompt 2:
Where is that pattern still showing up in your present life?

Prompt 3:
What would it mean to lay it down—and choose something new?

Breathe. Survival got you here. But healing will take you further.

**Whatever needs to come out—let it.
There's no wrong answer.**

DAY 42

Ritual Letter: To the One Who Kept Saying Sorry

This isn't just another prompt.
This is a ritual. A reckoning.
You're not journaling today—you're writing a letter.
Write to the version of you that kept apologizing just to survive.
The one who said "sorry" for asking, for crying, for taking up space.
The one who tried to stay small to stay safe.
Don't fix them.
Don't shame them.
See them.
You can comfort them.
You can rage with them.
You can thank them for keeping you alive.
But today, you tell them the truth:
You don't have to apologize for existing anymore.

Your ritual:
Write a letter to the you who kept saying "I'm sorry."
Tell them what they deserved to hear.
Use the next page.

Breathe. This is the moment your voice starts to come back.

This page is for the version of you that's always sorry.

DAY 43

What Truth Have You Been Avoiding Because It Would Change Everything?

Some truths feel like avalanches.
We tiptoe around them—because once we say them,
something breaks.
Or ends. Or begins.
But unspoken truth still shapes your life.
It weighs down your breath.
It speaks through silence.
It decides for you—until you decide to face it.
Today's not about solving it. It's about seeing it.

Reflective Prompts:

Prompt 1:
What's a truth you've been afraid to name—because of what it might change?

Prompt 2:
What do you fear would happen if you fully accepted it?

Prompt 3:
What would it mean to face it anyway?

Breathe. You don't have to fix it yet. Just name it. That's how truth becomes a doorway.

**Whatever needs to come out—let it.
There's no wrong answer.**

DAY 44

What Are You Still Trying to Earn?

Some part of you still thinks love must be earned.
Through silence.
Through sacrifice.
Through perfection.
But love that has to be earned isn't love. It's performance.
And the longer you perform, the more you disappear.
Today's about pulling back the curtain.
Seeing what part of you still believes you're not enough on your own.

Reflective Prompts:

Prompt 1:
What do you still find yourself working for in relationships—affection, validation, permission, peace?

Prompt 2:
When did you first start believing you had to earn love?

Prompt 3:
What would it feel like to stop performing? (Who would that version of you be?)

Breathe. You're not too much. You don't have to shrink to belong.

**Whatever needs to come out—let it.
There's no wrong answer.**

DAY 45

What Have You Normalized That Was Never Okay?

Some of the worst things that happened to you
never even registered as harm—
because they were *normal* where you came from.
You didn't know you could question it.
You thought you had to accept it. So you did. But survival isn't consent.
And just because you learned to live with it that doesn't mean it was ever fair.
Today is about seeing the harm that hid in plain sight.

Reflective Prompts:

Prompt 1:
What's something you used to think was normal—but now realize was hurtful?

Prompt 2:
How did adapting to that shape who you became?

Prompt 3:
If you were allowed to say, *"That wasn't okay,"* what would change?

Breathe. Your silence wasn't weakness. It was a strategy.
But you don't have to carry the weight of that silence forever.

**Whatever needs to come out—let it.
There's no wrong answer.**

DAY 46

What Were You Taught You Had to Earn?

Some of us were taught that love is a reward.
That safety has to be deserved. That rest must be justified.
But the things you were told you had to earn were often the very things you needed to survive.
This is where the loop forms:
You chase something that should've been yours by birthright—
trying to *deserve* it, instead of realizing it was never yours to earn.
Today, we name the chase.

Reflective Prompts:

Prompt 1:
What basic human need were you taught to earn—love, attention, safety, affection?

Prompt 2:
Where do you still feel like you have to prove yourself to receive it?

Prompt 3:
What would change if you believed you were worthy of it now?

Breathe.
You don't have to keep performing for something that should've been given freely.
You're allowed to rest.

**Whatever needs to come out—let it.
There's no wrong answer.**

DAY 47

What Part of You Is Still Waiting to Be Chosen?

Sometimes the hardest thing to admit is that we still want to be chosen.
By a parent. By a partner.
By someone who never saw us clearly—
or saw us and walked away.
That ache doesn't mean you're broken.
It means you're human.
It means there's a part of you still waiting to feel worthy.
But you don't have to wait anymore. You can choose yourself first.

Reflective Prompts:

Prompt 1:
Is there a part of you that still longs to be seen, chosen, or validated? What does it look like?

Prompt 2:
Who or what are you still hoping will finally say yes to you?

Prompt 3:
If you chose yourself instead of waiting—what would that look like today?

Breathe. You're not too much for wanting to be chosen.
But you don't have to stay unchosen to protect the story.

**Whatever needs to come out—let it.
There's no wrong answer.**

DAY 48

What Have You Learned to Call "Normal"?

Not everything you've adapted to was healthy.
Not everything you've survived should've been acceptable.
But your brain called it normal—
because it had to.
When chaos is consistent, it becomes familiar.
When numbness is rewarded, it becomes safety.
And soon, we stop questioning the cost.
Today, you will.

Reflective Prompts:

Prompt 1:
What patterns, behaviors, or relationships have you accepted as "normal" that might not be?

Prompt 2:
Where do you think you first learned that this was how life was supposed to feel?

Prompt 3:
If "normal" didn't mean safe—but real—what would your life look like instead?

Breathe. You're allowed to unlearn what you called home.
Even if it meant survival once— you don't have to carry it forever.

**Whatever needs to come out—let it.
There's no wrong answer.**

DAY 49

Loop Pause: Name the Pattern Again

You've been watching yourself.
Noticing the habits, the reactions, the stories that rise without invitation.
Today isn't for unpacking a new loop.
It's for pausing and seeing how far you've come.
You're going to revisit a pattern you've already named.
Not to shame yourself—but to check your footing.
Is it still running you? Or are you ready to let it go?

Reflective Prompts:

Prompt 1:
What loop has been showing up the most lately?

Prompt 2:
How do you usually react when it appears?

Prompt 3:
What's one small thing you've done differently this time?

Breathe.
This isn't backsliding.
It's awareness.
And awareness is power.

**Whatever needs to come out—let it.
There's no wrong answer.**

DAY 50

What's Still Looping?

You've come a long way. But healing isn't linear—some loops linger.
They sneak in when you're tired.
They whisper louder when you're alone.
They make old stories feel real again, even when you *know* better.
This isn't failure. It's residue.
Sometimes the loop doesn't disappear.
It just gets quieter—until you're ready to let it go completely.
Today, you're going to name what's *still* looping. Not with shame. With honesty.

Reflective Prompts:

Prompt 1:
What loop do you notice still shows up, even after all this work?

Prompt 2:
When does it usually appear? What situations, people, or emotions seem to trigger it?

Prompt 3:
What part of you still believes that loop is protecting you?

Breathe. You're not failing.
You're circling the exit. That matters.

**Whatever needs to come out—let it.
There's no wrong answer.**

DAY 51

What Would You Choose If Fear Wasn't In Charge?

Fear is subtle. It dresses up as logic. It speaks in caution.
It says, ***"Be careful, don't ask for too much."***
But fear isn't always the wisest voice in the room.
It's just the loudest. Especially when you're getting close to something real.
Today, you're going to listen *underneath* the fear.
And ask:
If fear wasn't in charge—what would I choose instead?

Reflective Prompts:

Prompt 1:
What choice are you avoiding right now because fear is too loud?

Prompt 2:
What would you do if you believed the outcome would *work out*?

Prompt 3:
What's one small step you can take today that your fear would normally stop?

Breathe. Fear protected you once.
But you're not living that story anymore.

**Whatever needs to come out—let it.
There's no wrong answer.**

DAY 52

What Have You Outgrown, But Haven't Let Go?

Some things don't break.
They just get too small.
A relationship.
A habit.
A role you learned to play to keep the peace.
You don't fit inside it anymore—but you haven't walked away.
Why?
Today, you name what no longer fits.
And start to loosen your grip.

Reflective Prompts:

Prompt 1:
What part of your life feels too small for who you're becoming?

Prompt 2:
What's kept you from letting it go?

Prompt 3:
What would you gain if you released it—and what do you fear you'd lose?

Breathe. Outgrowing isn't failure. It's evolution.

**Whatever needs to come out—let it.
There's no wrong answer.**

DAY 53

What Role Have You Been Playing to Be Loved?

We all perform, sometimes.
To be needed. To be wanted.
To be safe.
Maybe you became the caretaker.
The rebel. The strong one.
The silent one.
The one who never needed help.
But love that requires a performance isn't love. It's survival.
Today, you look at the role you've been cast in—and ask if you still want to play it.

Reflective Prompts:

Prompt 1:
What role have you been performing in your relationships?

Prompt 2:
Where did that role come from—and who benefits from you staying in it?

Prompt 3:
Who might you be… if you stopped playing it?

Breathe. You're allowed to lay the script down.

**Whatever needs to come out—let it.
There's no wrong answer.**

DAY 54

What Have You Called Strength That Was Actually Fear?

Sometimes we call it "being strong."
But really, it was shutting down.
Pushing through.
Not letting anyone see us break.
Sometimes, the strongest thing you can do… is stop pretending you're not afraid.
Not to be weak.
But to be real.
Today is about naming the difference between endurance and embodiment.

Reflective Prompts:

Prompt 1:
When have you said "I'm strong," but what you really meant was "I'm scared"?

Prompt 2:
What did that version of "strength" cost you?

Prompt 3:
What would strength look like now—if it wasn't just surviving?

Breathe.
There's more to you than what you've had to carry.

**Whatever needs to come out—let it.
There's no wrong answer.**

DAY 55

What Haven't You Let Yourself Grieve?

Grief isn't just about death.
It's about the lives we never lived.
The apologies we never got.
The versions of ourselves we had to abandon just to keep going.
If you don't let yourself grieve, your nervous system keeps trying to protect a wound it's never allowed to feel.
Today, we grieve. Not to stay in pain—
But to stop pretending it didn't hurt.

Reflective Prompts:

Prompt 1:
What haven't you let yourself grieve—because it didn't "count" or "wasn't that bad"?

Prompt 2:
What would it feel like to admit that it *did* hurt?

Prompt 3:
What part of yourself still aches to be seen in that story?

Breathe.
You don't need permission to grieve what you lost. Only willingness to feel it.

**Whatever needs to come out—let it.
There's no wrong answer.**

DAY 56

Ritual Letter: To the One Who Stayed Too Long

This isn't a prompt.
It's a release.
Today, you write to the version of you who stayed in the wrong place…
with the wrong person…
wearing the wrong mask…
because they thought that's what they had to do to survive.
This isn't about blame.
It's about release.
Maybe they stayed in the job that killed their spirit.
Maybe they said "yes" when they wanted to run.
Maybe they kept loving someone who only loved the version of them that was easy to control.
You're going to write to them.
Not to punish.
But to finally set them free.

Instructions:

Write a letter to the version of you who overstayed their welcome in a place, a relationship, or a pattern.
What were they afraid of?
What were they hoping for?
What do you wish they knew?
What do they deserve to hear now?
Use the next page to write your letter.

Breathe.
This is the sound of a door closing.
That's how you start to open one for yourself.

This page is for the version of you that stayed too long.

DAY 57

What's No Longer Yours to Carry?

Not everything you've been holding is yours.
Some of it was handed to you:
Guilt. Responsibility. Shame. Other people's comfort.
And because you were taught to be quiet, to be good, to not make waves—
you carried it.
But not everything you carry belongs in your hands forever.
And not everything that breaks when you set it down was ever yours to fix.

Reflective Prompts:

Prompt 1:
What are you still carrying that no longer belongs to you?

Prompt 2:
Whose weight is it really?

Prompt 3:
What would it feel like to let it fall—just for a moment?

Breathe.
You weren't made to be a container for everyone else's pain.
You're allowed to make space for your own becoming.

**Whatever needs to come out—let it.
There's no wrong answer.**

DAY 58

Whose Voice Still Tells Your Story?

You were born with a voice. But somewhere along the way, it got rewritten.
By parents. By partners. By silence.
Now, when you speak to yourself, it's not always *you* speaking.
It's the echoes of what they said.
What they believed.
What they needed you to be.
Today is about noticing that voice. And deciding whether you still believe it.

Reflective Prompts:

Prompt 1:
When you think about who you are, whose voice do you hear?

Prompt 2:
What part of that voice no longer fits the person you're becoming?

Prompt 3:
If it were your voice alone, what would you say instead?

Breathe.
You don't have to keep narrating your life with someone else's words.
You're allowed to rewrite the story.

**Whatever needs to come out—let it.
There's no wrong answer.**

DAY 59

What Are You Still Waiting For Permission To Do?

Somewhere inside, you're still waiting.
For a sign. For approval.
For someone to tell you it's okay to stop surviving.
But no one is coming to save you.
And no one gets to grant you permission—except you.
Today is about naming what you've postponed. And why.
And what it might feel like to stop waiting.

Reflective Prompts:

Prompt 1:
What are you still waiting for permission to do, feel, or become?

Prompt 2:
Who taught you that you had to wait?

Prompt 3:
What would it mean to give yourself permission now?

Breathe.
You don't need to be chosen to choose yourself.
This gets to be the day you say yes.

**Whatever needs to come out—let it.
There's no wrong answer.**

DAY 60

Mirror Page — Who Are You Becoming?

Look at how far you've come.
You've shed illusions.

You've faced truths that scared you.
You've spoken what used to stay silent.
But this isn't the finish line.

This is the moment you begin again—without the old mask, the old story, or the weight that was never yours.
Becoming isn't about perfection.
It's about choice.

Mirror Letter

Write a letter to the version of you who's waiting on the other side of this work.
The one who tells the truth now.
The one who doesn't beg for scraps.
The one who shows up with softness *and* strength.
Don't wait to be ready.
Write it like you already are.

Breathe.
Becoming begins with permission—and you just gave it.

This page is for the version of you that you're becoming.

PART 3

THE BECOMING

You've unraveled the loops.
You've reckoned with the patterns.

Now, it's time to choose who you want to become.
This part isn't about fixing yourself.

It's about remembering who you were before you forgot.
You are not your survival.
You are not your silence.
You are not your shame.
You are the one who stayed.
You are the one who wrote.
You are the one who now gets to decide.

This part is the turning.
The choosing.
The becoming.

Breathe.
The loop doesn't end here.
But *you* do — the version that kept you safe.

Let's meet the one you're ready to become.

DAY 61

What Would Freedom Feel Like?

You've spent so long surviving, you might not know what freedom would even look like.
Not just escape. Not just relief.
But actual freedom. Freedom is choosing without fear.
Loving without pretending. Existing without apology.
Before you can live it, you have to imagine it.
Today, you begin that.

Reflective Prompts:

Prompt 1:
What does *freedom* mean to you—not in theory, but in your body?
(What would it feel like to wake up free?)

Prompt 2:
What loops would no longer run your life if you were truly free?

Prompt 3:
What's one small decision you could make today that moves you closer to that freedom?

Breathe.
You're not becoming someone new.
You're becoming someone true.

**Whatever needs to come out—let it.
There's no wrong answer.**

DAY 62

Who Taught You What Love Was Supposed to Feel Like?

Before you chose your relationships, someone else showed you what love looked like.
How it sounded. How it hurt.
How much of yourself you had to give up to keep it.
You learned love through experience—not truth.
And now, you get to unlearn.
Today is about noticing the blueprint you inherited,
so you can stop building houses that never feel like home.

Reflective Prompts:

Prompt 1:
Who first taught you what love felt like? What did that version of love require from you?

Prompt 2:
How have you recreated that version of love in your adult relationships?

Prompt 3:
What would it mean to love without those conditions now?

Breathe.
Love isn't supposed to feel like performance.
It's supposed to feel like peace.

**Whatever needs to come out—let it.
There's no wrong answer.**

DAY 63

Loop Pause: What Loop Still Has a Hold on You?

You've named the patterns. You've broken some. But not all of them let go so easily.
Some loops stay quiet—until something shakes.
Then they reappear, like ghosts. You may have even felt one tugging at you recently.
The one that says, "You're not ready." "You'll mess this up." "It's safer not to try."
This page isn't about fixing it. It's about witnessing it—without judgment.
Because if a loop is still showing up, it means it still believes it's keeping you safe.
But safety isn't the same as becoming.

Reflective Prompts:

Prompt 1:
What loop still tugs at you when you're afraid or uncertain?

Prompt 2:
What part of you still believes this loop is protecting you?

Prompt 3:
If you chose to let that loop go today, what would feel most unfamiliar—or free?

Breathe. You're not failing.
You're just facing the next layer.
That's how healing works.

**Whatever needs to come out—let it.
There's no wrong answer.**

DAY 64

Where Do You Still Feel Like You're Too Much?

There's a difference between being *too much* and being *too aware of how much others can't hold you*.
The world may have told you you're intense.
Dramatic. Hard to love. But maybe it was never you.
Maybe it was the absence of people who could meet you.
Today, you're not shrinking to fit.
You're making space for the whole of you.

Reflective Prompts:

Prompt 1:
When was the first time someone told you that you were "too much"?
What part of you were they really responding to?

Prompt 2:
Where do you still feel like you have to dim yourself to be accepted?

Prompt 3:
What would it look like to stop apologizing for your depth?

Breathe.
Intensity is not a flaw.
It's your signal that you're still alive.
Don't water yourself down.

**Whatever needs to come out—let it.
There's no wrong answer.**

DAY 65

What Version of You Are You Afraid to Outgrow?

Sometimes the pain isn't from who you were…
It's from what you had to become in order to survive.
Even when you're ready to heal, part of you hesitates—
because that version of you got you through.
They held the line. They didn't fold. They protected you when no one else did.
But they aren't the only you. And they don't have to keep carrying it.
Today, you get to grieve the one who kept you safe— so you can become the one who knows how to live.

Reflective Prompts:

Prompt 1:
What version of you do you know you've outgrown—but still feel loyal to?

Prompt 2:
What did they protect you from? What did they carry that you no longer have to?

Prompt 3:
What would it mean to thank them—and let them go?

Breathe.
Loyalty to pain isn't love.
It's time to love the one you're becoming.

**Whatever needs to come out—let it.
There's no wrong answer.**

DAY 66

What Have You Been Waiting For Permission To Do?

There's a version of you that's been waiting.
Waiting to speak. Waiting to leave.
Waiting to love without apology.
Waiting to rest without guilt.
Maybe you were taught to ask first.
Maybe you needed approval before taking up space.
But becoming means choosing yourself—
before someone else does it for you.
Today isn't about rebellion. It's about reclamation.

Reflective Prompts:

Prompt 1:
What's something you've wanted for a long time but still haven't let yourself have?

Prompt 2:
Whose permission are you still waiting for?

Prompt 3:
What would change if you gave that permission to yourself?

Breathe. You don't need to be chosen. You need to choose.

**Whatever needs to come out—let it.
There's no wrong answer.**

DAY 67

How Do You Want to Respond Instead?

Your old loops were reactions—
automatic, emotional, often protective.
You shut down. You lashed out. You ran. You pretended.
But becoming means you don't just react.
You respond. You choose.
Today, you get to rewrite the script—
not to erase who you were,
but to become who you meant to be all along.

Reflective Prompts:

Prompt 1:
Think of a moment recently when you reacted out of habit.
What happened? What did it cost you?

Prompt 2:
If you could replay that moment, how would you want to respond instead?

Prompt 3:
What would need to shift in you to make that response possible next time?

Breathe. You're not a reaction. You're a response in progress.

Whatever needs to come out—let it.
There's no wrong answer.

DAY 68

What Would It Feel Like to Trust Yourself Again?

For so long, you second-guessed everything.
You needed proof. Permission. Reassurance.
You learned not to trust yourself—
because someone taught you not to.
But what if that story is over?
Self-trust isn't built in one day.
It's built every time you choose to listen.
Every time you hear your voice and believe it.

Reflective Prompts:

Prompt 1:
When was the last time you ignored your gut—and regretted it? What did you learn?

Prompt 2:
What does your intuition sound like? How do you know it's yours?

Prompt 3:
What's one way you can honor your own voice today—out loud?

Breathe. You don't have to earn your voice.
You just have to hear it—and trust that it's real.

**Whatever needs to come out—let it.
There's no wrong answer.**

DAY 69

What If the Story Was Never True?

Some beliefs were planted in you—
not chosen by you.
Maybe you were told you were too much.
Too sensitive. Too selfish. Unlovable. Unfix-able.
You didn't agree at first.
But over time, you repeated them—until they felt like yours.
What if they were never true?

Reflective Prompts:

Prompt 1:
What's one belief you've carried about yourself that might not actually belong to you?

Prompt 2:
Where did it come from? Whose voice was it originally?

Prompt 3:
What truth are you ready to believe instead?

Breathe.
You don't owe your life to someone else's lie.
You get to tell a different story now.

**Whatever needs to come out—let it.
There's no wrong answer.**

Day 70

Ritual Letter: To the One You're Becoming

You've spent weeks unraveling your past and reckoning with your patterns.
Now, it's time to speak directly to the one you're stepping into.

This isn't about being "healed."
It's about being honest.

You don't have to have it all figured out.
You just have to be willing to become someone who doesn't pretend anymore.
Write a letter to the version of you who is waiting on the other side of the loop.
The one who lives without the mask.
The one who doesn't need permission to speak.
You can tell them what you hope for.

What you're scared of.
What you're still carrying—and what you're ready to leave behind.

Be honest.
Be messy.
Be real.

This is a promise, not a performance.

Use the space on the next page to write your letter.

Breathe.
This is your becoming.
It's not a finish line.
It's a beginning.

This page is for the version of you waiting on the other side.

DAY 71

What Are You No Longer Apologizing For?

Becoming isn't just about what you're growing into.
It's about what you're leaving behind.
Sometimes, growth looks like unapologetically claiming space you used to shrink from.
Sometimes, it sounds like silence—where you once would've over-explained yourself.
What if you didn't have to say sorry for simply being?
Today, you get to name the things you no longer apologize for.
Not out of defiance. But out of self-respect.

Reflective Prompts:

Prompt 1:
What is something you've always apologized for—whether with words or with behavior?

Prompt 2:
What do you think made you believe you had to?

Prompt 3:
What would your life feel like if you stopped apologizing for that?

Breathe. You are not a burden.
You are a body reclaiming space.

**Whatever needs to come out—let it.
There's no wrong answer.**

DAY 72

What Would It Mean to Trust Yourself Again?

Becoming yourself means becoming your own safe place.
But that's hard when you've broken your own trust before.
When you stayed too long. When you silenced your gut.
When you abandoned yourself for someone else.
Self-trust isn't a lightning strike. It's a rebuild.
Brick by brick. Boundary by boundary. Truth by truth.
You don't have to trust yourself fully today. But you can begin again.

Reflective Prompts:

Prompt 1:
When was the last time you felt like you couldn't trust yourself? What happened?

Prompt 2:
What would rebuilding that trust look like—realistically?

Prompt 3:
What's one promise you can make to yourself today—and keep?

Breathe.
Self-trust isn't a leap.
It's a return.

**Whatever needs to come out—let it.
There's no wrong answer.**

DAY 73

What Does Safe Feel Like—For Real?

Most people say they want safety.
But many don't know what that actually means.
They've learned to call numbness "calm."
They've mistaken chaos for connection.
They've called survival "strength."
Today is about learning what safety *actually* feels like—
in your body, your mind, your relationships, your space.
Because if you can't recognize it, you won't know how to choose it.

Reflective Prompts:

Prompt 1:
What have you previously called "safety" that wasn't?

Prompt 2:
What does safety feel like in your body, when it's real?

Prompt 3:
What would it mean to build a life that feels safe to return to?

Breathe.
You are allowed to build peace that doesn't feel like war.

**Whatever needs to come out—let it.
There's no wrong answer.**

DAY 74

What Boundary Are You Finally Ready to Hold?

Boundaries aren't walls. They're doors—with locks you choose.
They're how you say:
"This version of me is no longer up for negotiation."
But holding a boundary isn't just about others.
It's about the part of you that used to bend.
That said yes to be loved.
That tolerated what hurt because you didn't think you deserved better.
Today is about defining one boundary you're ready to keep— even if it shakes something loose.

Reflective Prompts:

Prompt 1:
What's a boundary you've struggled to keep in the past?

Prompt 2:
What did abandoning that boundary cost you?

Prompt 3:
What will it take to hold that boundary now—with love, not fear?

Breathe.
Your peace is worth protecting—even from old versions of you.

**Whatever needs to come out—let it.
There's no wrong answer.**

DAY 75

Which Part of You Still Doesn't Trust This?

Not every part of you made it to this day willingly.
Some pieces are still bracing.
Still doubting. Still whispering, "It won't last."
That voice isn't the enemy.
It's a version of you that remembers when hope hurt.
And you've survived long enough to understand why it learned to stay silent.
But now— you're allowed to turn toward it, not away.

Reflective Prompts:

Prompt 1:
Which part of you is still waiting for this to fall apart?

Prompt 2:
What is that part protecting you from?

Prompt 3:
How can you honor that part—without letting it run the show?

Breathe.
You can carry your fear without giving it the map.
This road belongs to the one who's becoming.

**Whatever needs to come out—let it.
There's no wrong answer.**

DAY 76

Where Did You Learn to Wait for Permission?

You weren't always cautious.
There was a time you just *moved*.
Spoke. Reached. Acted.
Before fear dressed itself as wisdom.
Somewhere along the way, you stopped asking what *you* wanted.
You started waiting for someone else to approve your next step.
To validate your worth. To give you permission to be free.
But becoming doesn't wait.

Reflective Prompts:

Prompt 1:
Where in your life are you still waiting for permission?

Prompt 2:
Whose voice taught you that you needed to wait?

Prompt 3:
What would you do if no one had to agree?

Breathe. This is your life.
You don't need a signature to start living it.

**Whatever needs to come out—let it.
There's no wrong answer.**

DAY 77

Loop Pause: What's Still Looping?

You've named the stories. You've peeled back the masks.
You've seen what survival taught you to hide.
But some loops don't break on the first try.
Some are sticky. Familiar. Seductive in their ache.
Today is for noticing what's still there. What's still pulling.
What still feels safe, even when it's hurting you. Not to judge. Not to force a breakthrough.
Just to pause. To listen. To see clearly what still needs to be seen.

Reflective Prompts:

Prompt 1:
What's one loop that still feels hard to let go of? What makes it feel safer than the unknown?

Prompt 2:
What would it cost you to finally break it? And what might it give you?

Prompt 3:
If you could speak to the part of you still running the loop, what would you say?

Breathe. You're not failing.
You're noticing.
And that's how loops begin to loosen.

**Whatever needs to come out—let it.
There's no wrong answer.**

DAY 78

What Are You Afraid Will Happen If You Change?

By now, you've seen the loops.

You've spoken to the masks. You've written letters no one else will ever read.

But sometimes, even with all that awareness… you still don't move.

Why? Because change isn't just hard. It's threatening.

Even pain can feel safer than freedom if freedom means risking the unknown.

So today, ask yourself:

What part of you is still clinging to the familiar, even though it hurts?

You don't have to let go yet. But you do have to tell the truth.

Reflective Prompts:

Prompt 1
What's one change you know you need to make, but haven't?

Prompt 2
What are you afraid will happen if you make that change?

Prompt 3
What if the fear is real—and you're still allowed to want more anyway?

Breathe.
Even if fear comes with you, you still get to choose where you're going.

**Whatever needs to come out—let it.
There's no wrong answer.**

DAY 79

What Are You Willing to Risk for Peace?
You say you want peace. But peace costs something.
It costs the performance. It costs the mask.
It costs your place in systems that only love you when you're suffering.
Peace asks for your honesty.
Your boundaries.
Your truth—even when it's inconvenient.
So today isn't just about desire. It's about decision.
What are you finally ready to stop sacrificing?

Reflective Prompts:
Prompt 1
Where in your life have you chosen comfort over peace?

Prompt 2
What would change if you risked being fully honest?

Prompt 3
What's one truth you're willing to stand in, even if it costs you something?

Breathe.
Peace doesn't arrive. It's built—one truth at a time.

**Whatever needs to come out—let it.
There's no wrong answer.**

DAY 80

What Part of You Still Believes You're Broken?

Healing isn't about becoming perfect.
It's about realizing you were never ruined to begin with.
But part of you might still believe it.
That you're too much. Too needy.
Too late. That part has a voice.
And today, you're going to let it speak.
Not to shame it—but to hear it clearly.
Because if you don't listen to it, it will keep running your life from the background.

Reflective Prompts:

Prompt 1
What part of you still feels unworthy of love or peace?

Prompt 2
Where did that belief come from? Whose voice does it sound like?

Prompt 3
What would you say to that part of you now, if you were the one offering safety?

Breathe.
The belief that you're broken isn't yours.
You get to leave it behind.

**Whatever needs to come out—let it.
There's no wrong answer.**

DAY 81

What Are You Still Apologizing For?

Some of your habits were born from survival. So were your apologies.
You apologized for being too quiet.
Too loud. Too emotional. Too unavailable.
But maybe what you were really doing… was just trying to belong.
Today's about noticing the places you still shrink.
The places you brace. The parts of you that say "sorry" just for existing.
Not to stop them—but to understand them.

Reflective Prompts:

Prompt 1
What's something you've apologized for recently that didn't need an apology?

Prompt 2
Where do you think that automatic apology came from?

Prompt 3
What would it feel like to stop apologizing for that part of you—and instead, let it be enough?

Breathe.
You're allowed to take up space.
You don't need permission to exist.

**Whatever needs to come out—let it.
There's no wrong answer.**

DAY 82

Where Have You Already Changed?

You've been so focused on what's left to fix,
you might've missed what's already different. Not everything is how it used to be.
Some reactions have softened. Some patterns didn't repeat.
Some truths were finally named.
Change doesn't always shout.
Sometimes, it whispers.
Today is for noticing the quiet progress.
The small revolutions. The evidence that you're already becoming.

Reflective Prompts:

Prompt 1
What's something you've handled differently recently—compared to how you would've in the past?

Prompt 2
What changed in you that allowed that new response?

Prompt 3
What part of yourself are you starting to trust more?

Breathe. You've already begun.
You don't need to become someone else—just more of who you truly are.

**Whatever needs to come out—let it.
There's no wrong answer.**

DAY 83

What No Longer Fits?

Growth means shedding.
Some stories… Some habits… Some relationships…
Some identities—They only made sense inside the loop.
But you're not in the loop anymore. You don't have to keep proving what you've outgrown.
You don't have to keep shrinking into what once felt safe.
Not everything that carried you was meant to stay.
Today is for releasing what doesn't fit the version of you you're becoming.

Reflective Prompts:

Prompt 1
What's something you've been holding onto out of habit—but deep down, you know it no longer serves you?

Prompt 2
Why has it been hard to let that go?

Prompt 3
What would it look like to gently release it—without shame?

Breathe. You're not abandoning yourself.
You're making room for who you are now.

**Whatever needs to come out—let it.
There's no wrong answer.**

DAY 84
Ritual Letter: To the One Who Will Be Remembered

This isn't just a prompt.
It's a legacy.

Today, you're going to write a letter to the version of you the world will remember—not the one who survived, but the one who chose.

The one who said the hard truth.
The one who broke the cycle.
The one who loved anyway.

This letter is for the you who kept becoming, even when no one else was watching.
You're not writing this for praise.
You're writing it because you need to know what you're building.

So tell them:
Who were you when no one was looking?
What do you want your name to mean when you're gone?
What do you hope your life teaches others to choose?

Use the next page to write a letter to the version of you who becomes a story worth telling.

Write it like you mean it.
Because you're still writing it every day.

This page is for the version of that will be remembered.

DAY 85

What Parts of You Were Never Broken—Just Buried?

Healing isn't always about fixing what's wrong.
Sometimes it's about recovering what was never truly lost—just hidden.
There were parts of you that knew joy before you were taught to feel shame.
Parts that trusted before they learned to perform.
Parts that spoke boldly before silence became survival.
Today isn't about grief.
It's about excavation.

Reflective Prompts:

Prompt 1:
What qualities did you have before the world taught you to be someone else?

Prompt 2:
Which parts of you have you mistaken as "broken"—but were actually buried?

Prompt 3:
How might you begin to unearth and embody them again?

Breathe.
You're not rebuilding.
You're reclaiming. Let what was buried speak.

**Whatever needs to come out—let it.
There's no wrong answer.**

DAY 86

What Do You Want Your Voice to Sound Like Now?

You've spoken from survival.
From silence.
From the stories others gave you.
But now, your voice is yours again.
Not the one that begged to be heard.
The one that speaks because it knows it belongs.
This isn't about being loud. It's about being true.

Reflective Prompts:

Prompt 1:
When you imagine your truest voice, what does it sound like? (Calm? Unapologetic? Curious?)

Prompt 2:
What's one thing your voice hasn't said out loud—because it didn't feel safe enough?

Prompt 3:
How can you begin using your voice in a way that reflects who you're becoming?

Breathe.
You don't have to shout to be heard.
You just have to speak from who you are.

**Whatever needs to come out—let it.
There's no wrong answer.**

DAY 87

Where Are You Still Performing?

Not every mask gets thrown off at once.
Some of them still feel useful. Some of them still protect you in certain rooms.
But protection has a cost:
You disappear again.
This part of your journey isn't about perfection.
It's about awareness.
Noticing when you slip back into the old self— And choosing to return.

Reflective Prompts:

Prompt 1:
Where in your life do you still feel the need to perform?

Prompt 2:
What version of you shows up in those moments—and who are they trying to please?

Prompt 3:
What would it look like to stay with your real self instead?

Breathe.
You don't need to become someone else to belong.
You already do.

**Whatever needs to come out—let it.
There's no wrong answer.**

DAY 88

What Do You Actually Want?

Not what's safe. Not what's reasonable. Not what they told you to want.
What do you want?
Desire is not selfish. It's a compass.
And for too long, you've been surviving by giving up yours.
Today, you listen.
Not to the critic. Not to the fear. To the whisper underneath all that noise.

Reflective Prompts:

Prompt 1:
If you could want without apology, what would you ask for?

Prompt 2:
Whose voice taught you that your wants were "too much"?

Prompt 3:
What's one small way you can start choosing your desire today?

Breathe.
Desire doesn't make you selfish.
It makes you sovereign.

**Whatever needs to come out—let it.
There's no wrong answer.**

DAY 89

What Are You Still Waiting For Permission To Do?

Most of us were taught to wait.
For approval. For the "right" time.
For someone to say it's okay to want more.
But no one's coming to give you permission.
That's your job now.
This isn't about recklessness.
It's about reclamation.
Because waiting is just another kind of silence.

Reflective Prompts:

Prompt 1:
What are you still waiting for permission to feel, want, or do?

Prompt 2:
Whose approval are you still chasing—or avoiding?

Prompt 3:
What would change if you gave yourself that permission right now?

Breathe. You don't need anyone else's okay.
You're the one writing the rules now.

**Whatever needs to come out—let it.
There's no wrong answer.**

DAY 90

Mirror Page: This Is Who I Am Now

Look at what you've done.
Not just the pages filled.

But the parts of you you've faced.
You didn't skip the hard truths.
You didn't run from the loops.

You stayed. You softened. You became.

This isn't the end of your healing.
It's the end of hiding.
The end of waiting.
The end of becoming someone else just to be loved.

Today, you meet yourself without the mask.

Mirror Letter

Write a letter to the version of you who made it here.
The one who didn't give up.

The one who chose to feel, to reflect, to become.
You don't need to fix anything.
You don't need to prove anything.

Just witness what's changed.
Write it all down.

Not because it's done—
but because now,
you finally know who you are.

Use the next page to write the letter to yourself who never gave up and wont give up from here.

Breathe.
You did it.
Welcome home, Loopbreaker.

This page is for the version of you that didn't give up.

The Final Ritual

Looking Back To go Forward

Before you close this journal, take a few quiet minutes to turn through its pages.
Reread what you wrote on the days you almost quit, the ones you rushed through, and the ones that cracked something open.

Notice the handwriting shifts. The tone changes. The way your words softened when you started telling the truth.

Let yourself *see* the work you've done. Not to judge it—just to witness it.

Every page in here is proof that you stayed.
Every reflection is evidence of becoming.

When you reach the beginning again, pause on that first entry.
Read it as the version of you who exists *now*.

Breathe in the difference.
Feel the distance between who began and who arrived.

Then close the book gently and say it out loud, one last time:

"I stayed."

That's the ritual.
That's the work.
That's the becoming.

This is Not the End

You've made it through all 90 days.
Not because you had to.
Because something in you knew it was time.

You've met the voice in your head.
You've met the one beneath it.
And maybe, for the first time, you've met yourself.

This is not the end.
It's the first day of listening differently.
Of living in your voice.
Of breaking the loop—one choice at a time.

Welcome home, LoopBreaker.

We'll see you in the mirror.

LoopBreaker Next Steps

This journal was the mirror. Now the voice speaks back.

If something cracked open in these pages—
If you found a part of yourself you weren't ready to name—
If you wrote something you didn't know you believed—

You're not alone.
This isn't the end of the loop.
It's the start of the rewrite.
The work doesn't end here. It just goes deeper.
And you don't have to do it alone.

We're building a tribe of LoopBreakers..
People who are choosing to live with their eyes open— even when it costs everything.
I'm not offering a brand.
I'm offering a mirror, a drumbeat, and a place to walk alongside others doing the same.
You'll find me here:

Podcast: voiceinyourhead.org

IG: @im_the_voice_in_your_head_

FB: *The Voice in Your Head*

TikTok: @voice_in_your_head_

Come as you are. Stay if it's true. Bring your voice.
I truly appreciate you. Rest well, LoopBreaker.
You've earned it.
-Noah

You've just heard the Voice in Your Head.

WANT TO HOLD THE MIRROR LONGER?

The LoopBreaker Reflection Deck is coming soon.
As well as more tailored iterations of these journals.
I hope to make one specific to your struggles!
You're not just healing.
You're becoming.
Welcome to the mirror.

Want to go Deeper?

The Voice in Your Head
A Reckoning. A Mirror. A Beginning.
You've broken loops.
You've met yourself on the page.
Now go deeper.

The Voice in Your Head isn't a workbook.
It's the book that started it all —
a haunting, a guide, a reflection that cuts past masks and straight into truth.
- Raw, trauma-informed insights
- Stories that mirror your survival self
- Tools to rewire your nervous system and reclaim your voice

Available now wherever books are sold.
ISBN: 979-8-9993026-0-1
By Noah Wraith · Published by OneVoiceOS LLC

www.ingramcontent.com/pod-product-compliance
Lightning Source LLC
LaVergne TN
LVHW070530070526
838199LV00075B/6746